PLANET IN REBELLION
A Cosmic Look at Earth's History

Joy Furuta

Copyright 2015 Joy Furuta

ISBN# 978-1-941052-12-9 Trade Paper
Library of Congress Control Number: 2015951902

Cover Design: Antelope Design
Cover Photo: Courtesy NASA

All rights reserved.
No part of this book may be reproduced or
transmitted in any form or by any means,
electronic or mechanical, including photocopying,
recording or by any information storage and retrieval
system without written permission from the publisher.

An imprint of Pronghorn Press
PronghornPress.org

Table of Contents

Preface   7

1
Introductions to Those Presenting These Materials   11

2
The Conceptual Design of Earth   17

3
In the Beginning   24

4
How the Planet was Taken Off-Course   31

5
The Results
of
Being Taken Off-Course 43

6
The Current Impacts
of
Being Off-Course 59

7
Moving to the Present 68

8
Anticipation of the Future 87

9
The Return to the Divine Path 93

Index 97

*To all the Lightworkers—
May you celebrate your accomplishments*

A Cosmic Look at Earth's History

Preface

I am fascinated by the way that reality is created; I spent my youth reading the myths of the world, and my adult years reading science fiction. I have constantly looked for information about this, and I devoured the Seth books when I discovered them.

I have always been sensitive to input from the beyond. As a result of this, some nonphysical entities that I was working with taught me how to telepathically communicate with them. Imagine my delight with this direct access to information from the other side of the veil. Consequently, I've asked a fairly

A Cosmic Look at Earth's History

constant stream of questions that has lead to information from a wide variety of sources.

I work with a number of nonphysical beings. Recently they told me that because of the vibrational changes brought about by this planet's entry into new era at the end of 2012, the planet is being removed from quarantine. Since I did not know that Earth was in quarantine, this piqued my interest, so I asked questions.

Quarantine means that Earth has been isolated from interactions with other planets and beings in the universe. Therefore, it does not receive many of the energies that are provided to other planets with physical life upon them. Many of these energies are connective, and spiritual in origin. An example is communications with other planets. Lack of communications has led those now alive to believe that Earth is the only planet with intelligent life upon it.

I learned that Earth had been placed in quarantine around 500,000 years ago due to the impact of Lucifer's actions on this planet. This information surprised me because I grew up believing that Lucifer was a myth. I was stunned to learn that he had a strong impact on the development of the life on this planet, and on the planet itself. The result of those actions is that Earth is classified as a planet in rebellion.

The questions that I asked of those I work with provided a broader picture of what has happened to this planet, and what is now anticipated to be happening in the not too distant future. I share this information with you for your edification.

A Cosmic Look at Earth's History

1

INTRODUCTIONS TO THOSE PRESENTING THESE MATERIALS

We greet you. We are a variety of beings that are working with the one channeling this material, Joy, to bring you information on the past of this planet, and on the new future now unfolding. This new future promises to be exciting, rewarding, and fulfilling. In the future we see developing, we expect that finally you will be able to live your lives in many of the ways that you have always desired, and have not been able to actualize in your past lives.

A Cosmic Look at Earth's History

Let us begin with some introductions as to who we are.

GAIA

I greet you. I am Gaia. I am the soul of this planet.

You also know me by many other names; among these are Mother Earth, and Mother Nature. I truly enjoy being your host, and I am truly enjoying the experiences that you now bring, the experience of ascension of both the planet and mankind. I love you dearly, and I wish for you to carry this knowledge with you in your hearts at all times.

HOSTS OF HEAVEN

We greet you. We are the Hosts of Heaven. We are also called the Archangels by your religious institutions.

We are here to support all intelligent life upon the planet, and the planet herself. We

PLANET IN REBELLION

have been intimately involved in the evolution of this planet, and in the lives of each of you who reads these materials. Each of you has an Archangel that accompanies you throughout all of your lives upon the planet. This angel assists you in all that you seek to do upon the planet that uplifts the planet or yourself. You can call upon your Archangel at any time to assist you. Your Archangel looks forward to a deeper and more conscious interaction with you.

LORD MICHAEL

I greet you. I am the Lord and god of this planet. You may call me Lord Michael.

In presenting these materials, I seek to broaden your understanding of what you and your planet have endured over many long eons of time. By your desires and your actions, you have succeeded in pulling the vibrations of this planet up to the point where it is now moving out of the rebellion it entered 500,000 years ago. Therefore, we have now entered a time in which it is appropriate to look back on the rebellion started by Lucifer and your planetary ruler and see how it has affected you. For now you begin the joyful task of healing these wounds, and rediscovering the love that my father, the Creator, has always had for you, and will always have for you.

I give you my love, and I thank you for considering these materials.

OKAHTIER

I greet you. I call myself Okahtier, which translates to "honored, spirit architect." I am Joy's soul.

I have had a long and illustrious association with this planet. At one time I was one of Gaia's Devas. I designed lifeforms that existed on the planet and I specialized in trees. When it became appropriate, I left that role to begin incarnating as a human upon the planet. Joy is the latest of my creations, and I love her dearly.

PLANET IN REBELLION

SATAMBUSEENO

I greet you. I am the one who is called Satambuseeno.

I am one that has come to join you in this time of momentous change on the planet. I am here to assist you in the movement out of rebellion and into an orderly progression forward to the realization of the love of the Creator. Originally, I came from a planet that had rebelled in a galaxy far away from your planet. I was fortunate to be born at the time my home planet was beginning its movement out of the disruptive patterns of rebellion. As a result of that life, I became fascinated with this process. I have spent much of the time from that lifetime until now studying how rebellion affects those living on a planet, and the process of healing those impacts. I look forward to interacting with many of those who read these materials. You may call upon me at any time to aid and assist you.

ST. GERMAIN

I greet you. I call myself St. Germain because I believe that I am always germane or pertinent.

I have lived many lives upon the Earth. I appeared in your Christian scriptures as Samuel. Most recently I was known as Mark Twain.

I have vast experience in the conditions that humans experience, and I desire to bring you my understanding of how you can move beyond your currently perceived limitations.

2

THE CONCEPTUAL DESIGN
OF
EARTH

To begin with, let's discuss Earth from the viewpoint of the non-physical. We will start with the conceptual underpinnings of this planet.

THE
EVOLUTIONARY PLANETARY DESIGN

I greet you. This is Lord Michael. I am the god of your planet.

A Cosmic Look at Earth's History

One of my duties was to design that which I desired this planet to embody, and the particular types of experiences—and therefore the particular types of realizations—that come from those experiences.

There are a number of things that I incorporated in this design. The first of these was determining what will be explored. Human beings are experiencing life from the emotional, spiritual, physical, and mental points of view. The intent was that all of these factors would marry into one being who is capable of a wide variety of experiences and responses.

You who live on this planet believe intelligent life must embody all of these characteristics. Eventually, you will find that having the ability to experience your life from all these vantage points is very rare within Creation.

There are many lifeforms that understand the mental point of view, and there are fewer lifeforms that understand the emotional point of view. Because I desired this planet to explore life from all these points of view, this was one of the primary factors in the blueprint.

PLANET IN REBELLION

The next way in which I desired you to experience life is in the context of duality, the context of male and female. This you also take for granted as the norm for an intelligent species. There are many other ways that reproduction can occur that were not chosen. One of these that is well known to you is the direct duplication of the existing adult. You see many of your simpler lifeforms, such as the amoeba, reproducing in this fashion.

The design also included instructions as to how I expected you to evolve. I had selected a gradual coming to terms of all your abilities at the same time in each being. What you have now is specific abilities being developed in different groups.

For example, you have the physical abilities being developed in your athletes, and you have the mental abilities being developed in your scholars. But rarely is an athlete a scholar, and vice versa. Therefore, the merging of these abilities is currently left to future generations to enact.

And finally, the design I created contained directions on how I wished for you to discover the love of the Creator. Again, this was to be a gradual reconnection to the overwhelming love that exists for all life. This will be one of the places where the planet has moved the most off-course. The rediscovery of this universal love will bring about the greatest changes that this planet has ever seen.

THE FOUR BODY SYSTEM

I greet you. This is Gaia.

I am very pleased to be discussing the past with you. Many of you who are now reading these materials remember much of this past. You have been alive before on this planet, and you will live here again. You have had much to do with the shaping of how the past has played out, for in many of your past lives you have been the movers and shakers who determined the course of history.

PLANET IN REBELLION

The Earth was designed to be a place where souls could gain experience from a multitude of directions at the same time. Each human being encompasses four different ways of experiencing. One teacher named Vywamus describes these multiple points of view as the four-body system with the following components.

You can experience from:

1. Emotional point of view

2. Intellectual point of view (which is largely conceptual)

3. Spiritual point of view

4. Physical point of view

You look at each of these from a male or active side, or from a female, or receptive side. You gain a greater understanding of what happened during an event when you seek to marry or integrate these multiple points of view.

A Cosmic Look at Earth's History

The history of this planet can also be viewed from these viewpoints:

• The physical history of mankind on the planet can be found in the writings of your archaeologists and anthropologists. They interpret their discoveries to give you a view into the past.

• Part of the spiritual history of the planet is contained within the teachings of your many religions. Given that the planet is designed to be experienced from multiple directions, if you as a people sought to marry the viewpoints of your many religions, you would find that you would gain a far greater understanding of your spirituality and the spirituality of the planet. Other parts of the spiritual history of the planet remain to be revealed in the times to come.

• The emotional history of the planet is in many ways encompassed by your interpretations of the many wars fought upon the planet. Although the justification for warfare is typically given as a desire for resources or territory, the energetic cause frequently comes down to some sort of emotional imbalance within a people, which causes them to go to war.

Additionally, you may look at many of your traditions concerning love, and the types of love contained within your family groups, for much more of the emotional history of the planet. It will not be straightforward to decipher this information, but then deciphering emotions in general is not straightforward for most people.

• The intellectual or conceptual history of the planet is what is taught to you in your schools. Whether or not these teachings are accurate can depend on how much of the other points of view outlined above are contained within those teachings.

3

IN THE BEGINNING

THE HISTORY OF THE PLANET BEFORE THE REBELLION

I greet you. This is Okahtier.

We will continue our narration of the events that happened so long ago on this planet. I have volunteered to present this next piece as I was instrumental in that time period.
Before we discuss history, let's discuss some of those responsible for the planet. Your planet has a hierarchy responsible for its progress and growth. Each of these will

be mentioned at some point. A partial list is as follows:

- Soul of the Planet. This one, whom you call Gaia or Mother Nature, embodies the physical structure of the planet. She holds the intent for physical life to exist here.

- Planetary Prince. This being is directly responsible for the day-to-day life here on the surface of the planet. Your original Planetary Prince fell to Lucifer and has been replaced by one who cares deeply for you.

- God. This one has introduced himself as Lord Michael, god of your planet. He is the designer of the planet, and he is the one who makes all changes to the design or blueprint of the planet.

- Creator. This one is the father of Lord Michael. In the concepts of God as defined by your current religions, the Creator and God are presented as one.

A Cosmic Look at Earth's History

We have discussed some of the conceptual underpinnings of Earth. Each planet in Creation that has intelligent life has a design, a blueprint. This contains directives for the planet, for the types of experiences which are available there, and for how it will evolve.

As described above, Earth's directives were ambitious. As you well know, ambitious plans can lead to spectacular successes, and to interesting diversions from the route planned for success. And this is what has happened here.

Life was progressing well under the designed blueprint which, by the way, was quite skillfully designed and thought out. The human species had evolved to the point where they were ready to start their spiritual evolution. This was the point in time when your anthropologists find that primates suddenly started developing tools, indicating a level of conceptual thinking which was not possible before that point in time.

Additional off-planet beings, and non-physical entities were being introduced to the human species to begin their long evolutionary education process. Those on the planet who accepted these new teachers made sudden leaps of development. Those who did not, died off fairly quickly. Therefore, the human race was making excellent progress, and all prognoses were for a smooth and successful evolutionary path.

It was at this point in time that your Planetary Prince succumbed to the teachings of the one called Lucifer. As discussed below, Lucifer was the ruler of the system to which this planet belongs. What Lucifer offered your Planetary Prince was a way to shortcut the developmental path. Keep in mind that the planet had already existed for millions of years, and it was then at the beginning point of its spiritual evolution.

I will let Lord Michael continue with this narration.

A Cosmic Look at Earth's History

OVERVIEW OF LUCIFER

I greet you. This is Lord Michael.

Since Lucifer is central to much of what happened here, let's discuss a bit of who he was.

Lucifer was a brilliant being who existed fairly high up in the administration of this universe. He oversaw many of the activities of my realm, including many of the activities of the development of your planet Earth.

As I've noted above, Lucifer was brilliant, both intellectually, and visually. He was charismatic and highly capable of understanding how to implement the desires of the infinite spirit and the Creator. And this brilliance of his shone forth from his being. You would say that he was the type of that lights up a room when he enters the party.

Because Lucifer was brilliant, he had

little understanding or compassion for those who needed to take a slower route to the ends that he could so clearly see in front of them. Therefore, Lucifer sought to speed up the evolution of this planet. And in doing so, he departed from Earth's evolutionary plans.

After Lucifer departed from Earth's designed path, he attracted a number of followers whose names you still know. The primary one of these is Satan.

At one time, Satan was Lucifer's principal assistant. Satan succumbed to Lucifer's insistent arguments regarding the validity of his desired course of action. Since that time, Satan has served as Lucifer's primary defender, and implementer of Lucifer's plans. At this time, the movements of both Lucifer and Satan have been restricted to a different planet. You will hear from neither of them ever again.

We have determined in the time since the events narrated in this document, Lucifer had a fatal flaw. This flaw was that he could not fully feel the love of the Creator, and the love that the Creator imbues all things that exist. This flaw led to excessive pride in his intellectual accomplishments. Most of you have met people of this sort. While they are interesting and fun to be with in a social setting, they are difficult to live with in the long run because they cannot love. And this has turned out to be the issue with Lucifer.

4

How the Planet was Taken Off-Course

I greet you. This is the Lord Michael.

Gaia has given you an overview of the intent of the design of this planet where you live. I will continue with these materials.

As Gaia has mentioned, the design of this planet was ambitious. It was intended to provide souls with comprehensive knowledge of physical experience by allowing them to look at their experiences on the planet from multiple points of view, and thereby gain much growth.

However, the sheer complexity of this design also gave those who did not desire to grow from their experiences many avenues to block the growth of those who sought to experience physical life in the designed ways. These forms of interference had many points of origin.

One of the primary sources was the interference of the one known as Lucifer. Lucifer was a brilliant being of great gifts and knowledge. He was given rulership over this part of the universe with the intent that he would oversee the progressive evolution of this ambitious planet. Lucifer performed admirably in many ways in that role for quite some time. However, at some point, Lucifer decided that the progress here was not fast enough.

Under normal circumstances this change of direction would not be difficult to compensate for, but the structure of what was being attempted on Earth was complex, and therefore the departure from that plan caused the planet to begin to swing more and more widely out of sync.

This meant that the planet began to explore a different evolutionary path, and the new path needed to be played through to the end before the planet could return to an understanding of what it was designed to experience.

We are now at the end of this path of diversion, and you and your children are beginning the task of returning this planet to its divine position in the universe.

THE ROLE OF LUCIFER

I greet you. My name is Satambuseeno.

I will continue this with a short description of the impacts that Lucifer and his followers have had on this planet.

I also come from a planet that has experienced rebellion. This is what Lucifer's actions amounted to: a rebellion against the divine plan for the evolution of Earth. Lucifer originally had good intent in his desires, and therefore his departure from the plans laid for this planet were for reasons of good intent.

It was very clear to many of those

involved with this planet, that its design was ambitious and therefore the plans were complex and elaborate. Because the steps were complicated, long stretches of time were built into the plans to allow those incarnating time to execute and assimilate each step.

This is the part that Lucifer sought to shorten. When he did so, the planet began to plunge into chaos. There was not enough time for those living on the planet to understand exactly what they were experiencing, and what the goal of each step was. There was not enough time for the basis of the next step to be properly laid before the step was taken. Therefore, each step took those living on the planet farther and farther from the divine plans.

As a result, those then living on the planet no longer had an innate understanding of their connection to God, and deliberate errors could be introduced to their experiences. A deliberate error is one that seeks to further separate the human being from his/her development of the understanding of the love of the Creator, and the love of God.

Now at that point, Lucifer descended

into pride. He could not or would not see that the results of his actions created suffering for those he ruled. Instead, he sought to explain his actions as a shining example of how evolution could occur. Those who followed him were in many ways blinded by his brilliance, and they upheld his interpretations.

At that point, Lord Michael was faced with the choice to either cut short the activities of Lucifer, or to allow the new evolutionary path to play itself out.

We will let Lord Michael continue this narrative.

Lord Michael's Decision

I greet you. This is Lord Michael.

As Satambuseeno has narrated, I was faced with a important choice at that point. As I had little experience along those lines, I sought the wisdom of those that had been through that experience before me. I was uniformly advised that all beings must be allowed to experience the results of their choices. The costs of not allowing this to happen would be exponential in terms of suffering and the longevity of this new path. I was given examples of what had happened in other places. Therefore, I chose to uphold the tenants of free will; I chose to allow these actions to continue until the time that those incarnating on the planet had learned how to bring these actions to an end.

That time is now, and I am very proud of those of you that are now living on this planet, and what you have managed to accomplish.

THE SUBVERSION OF THE PLANETARY PRINCE

I greet you. This is Okahtier.

I am pleased to continue this conversation now. We left this at the point where Lucifer descended into error. At that point Lucifer sought companions to move along this new path with him. One of those that he managed to subvert was your Planetary Prince.

I understand that you do not currently know you have a Planetary Prince. This is to some large degree because of the actions of the one who previously held that position. Because you have lived for so long without conscious interactions with this being, part of what you do not understand is what this entity is supposed to do for you, and for the planet.

Earlier I listed a series of beings that have responsibility for many of the aspects of this planet. Some are responsible for the planet itself. Many are responsible for how life is supposed to be lived on the planet. Your Planetary Prince was one of these.

His primary role was to be the intermediary between those who have larger roles that they play, such as your god and those who actually incarnate upon the planet. His role was to implement the decisions of those with more responsibilities, and to act as your defender with these beings. He was supposed to make sure that no decisions were made in the larger realms that would adversely affect life upon this planet.

When your Planetary Prince was subverted by Lucifer, his role changed dramatically. Instead of acting as your defender, he began trying to undermine those living on the planet. This threw the planet into a state of confusion. The Planetary Prince, as part of his role, has wide access to all those alive on Earth. You have a saying, "Speak of the devil, and he appears." This is because the devil as recorded in your history was your Planetary Prince. And because this being had that role, he was linked to all those who live on the planet. Therefore, any mention of him, would automatically draw his attention, and most likely his presence.

Your Planetary Prince used this ability to sabotage those he interacted with. Those who were alive at that time could see that this being was greater than they were, and therefore they were inclined to believe his pronouncements, no matter the eventual cost.

There were many consequences from those actions of your Planetary Prince. The major one is that the planet was thrown off course from the developmental pattern designed for it by your god. At this point you do not actually realize that there was a pattern designed for this planet, and that it was supposed to easily and gently move you into an understanding of your place within Creation, and the love of your god for you. In the next section, we will discuss the results of this change of pathways.

I would like to add one last note to this material. Your Planetary Prince has been replaced by one who truly loves you, loves this planet, and has been working ceaselessly to bring it back into a confirmation of the divine love that the Creator holds for all of Creation. This happened quite some time ago, but it has taken this long for the actions of the new Planetary Prince to bring you to the point where you are now, the beginning of the joyous return to the divine path.

The Results of the Fall of the Planetary Prince

I greet you. This is your Lord Michael. I will continue this narration now.

As Okahtier has told you, your Planetary Prince was subverted by Lucifer. Lucifer did this by promising him a quick and easy route to completing his task of overseeing the evolution and advancement of this planet by following Lucifer's plan. In essence, Lucifer's plan as described above, was designed to shortcut the steps needed for the planet to evolve. It eliminated steps and educational activities, and shortcut the time frames needed for the population to adapt to the necessary changes.

Your Planetary Prince was looking ahead to the eons needed for this planet to evolve. He had already spent many years bringing the planet to the point where it was

PLANET IN REBELLION

ready to start its spiritual evolution, and the length of time needed for that evolution looked daunting. Therefore, your Planetary Prince succumbed to Lucifer's offerings.

Because the design of this planet was complex, much thought had gone into the design of its evolutionary path. Consequently, when your Planetary Prince departed from the blueprint, there was very little I could do to compensate. Unfortunately, because of the nature of this change of plans, I had to isolate Earth. This meant that I put the planet into quarantine.

The people then alive quickly fell into disarray and warfare. You now believe that constant warfare is natural to the human species, and is to be expected. This was not the case at the time your Planetary Prince fell. Then, the existing cultures were matrilineal and peaceful in nature. Differences between humans were honored, with many techniques being taught to the children of how to resolve their conflicts in mutually beneficial ways. If those of you now alive were born into those times, you would consider that you had arrived in heaven on Earth.

Yet to those alive then, there was so

much more that they saw as potentials they could achieve, and that they desired. You also desire many of these same things, such as a greater connection to your Creator, but these desires have been hidden in many ways from your consciousness. However, they are still active within you, and you have been consistent in trying to achieve these for yourselves.

5

THE RESULTS
OF
BEING TAKEN OFF-COURSE

I greet you. This is Okahtier.

When we left our narration of things that happened in the distant past of this planet, your Planetary Prince had been subverted by Lucifer into abandoning Earth's designed evolutionary path. Gaia and company could have dealt with this alteration if it had not been accompanied by a strong dose of pride on the part of those seeking to move this planet onto a new evolutionary path. They believed they understood more about what was needed to evolve spiritually, and they were not willing to listen to the words or experiences of others, including that of your god.

Therefore, they somewhat willfully began to take apart the social structures that had already been accepted by those living on the planet, and to try to implement new ones to replace them.

Those new social structures were designed for a race that had evolved quite a bit farther than yours had at that time, and the new social structures did not work because the people did not understand what they were being asked to do. And so the people abandoned all social structures, and fell into warring with each other, attempting to gain by force that which they did not understand how to gain by negotiation or cooperation.

Those responsible for these changes did not want to accept that their grand new plan was not working. (You see vestiges of this type of behavior in modern times with the constant back and forths of your political parties.) They fell into disarray among themselves, with their only cooperative defensive point being the continued implementation of their plan. They started to reflect the energies of the peoples then alive, which was a lowering of their energetic set points. This de-evolution caused many of them to descend into cruel behaviors as a way of increasing their sense of self worth in their own eyes.

You have existed with this form of disarray for many eons. The results of this are many behaviors that you consider to be normal.

We will let the Archangels continue.

Human Nature

We greet you. We are the Hosts of Heaven. We will present the next part of this narration.

As you have been informed, your planet was somewhat forcefully taken off of its intended course. We, your supporters and companions, have intimately felt the distress and distortions that this detour has cost you. There are many things that you take as given these days that were not intended for you to ever experience. Some have resulted in behaviors that have caused you and the planet much distress, behaviors you take to be common and expected. You call many of them human nature.

You will be surprised to learn these behaviors are not common on other inhabited planets, or natural to you as a species. Instead these are defensive reactions you have developed as a result of the pressures to which you have been subjected. Many of them are somewhat detrimental to your evolution as spiritual beings.

For example, one typical behavior that many on your planet indulge in is the emphasis on the self over the good of the planet or the group to which they belong. You see the results of this in the levels of pollution that exist in many places, and in the alterations made to your food and water supply for the profit of the few.

When you get down to the root causes of these detrimental behaviors, you will find much of the basis is a lack of belief in self worth, and their worth in the eyes of their creators and their gods. Because they do not believe they have any inherent worth, they do not promote actions that support the worth of others. Indeed, in many ways they are incapable of seeing that their actions cannot achieve this.

Many of you reading these materials believe that human nature is innate; this is inherent in the term that you use to describe these behavioral characteristics. And you would be shocked to find out that very little in the human being in innate. The ability to feel emotions, think, and to physically sense are innate. Very little beyond that is built into the human being. Therefore your beliefs in the inevitability of aggression, defense, and desire for power are the result of distortions of the original plan for evolution on this planet.

Many of you will be distressed by these notions. You have spent lifetimes working to eliminate these behaviors in yourselves, and still they reappear. We are now entering the age in which such behaviors will no longer be supported, and this is because of the rise in spiritual energies which you have managed to draw down to this planet.

You will find in your children a lack of desire to follow the behavior paths set by their ancestors. When these children are told to hate their neighbor because the neighbors' ancestors harmed their ancestors, they will refuse to cooperate. You should celebrate this for this truly is the end to war, and to many of the patterns of aggression on this planet.

KARMA

I greet you once again. This is Okahtier. I am pleased and honored to be contributing to this document at this time.

Where we left you, your planet was moving into a state of chaos because of the changes instigated by Lucifer and Satan. Among the changes were DNA changes that you are finally working your way through. These led to differences in how you experienced and retained information. For instance, it became much easier to interpret an event as negative, and as harmful to you. You leap to this conclusion somewhat automatically, and this is the result of DNA changes.

The multi-dimensional parts of you that enhance positive experiences and help you to throw off negative experiences were suppressed by those changes. As a result, you retained more and more negative experiences. This eventually led to the karmic system whereby those energies that you could not deal with at a given time were stored until you could potentially deal with them. This also led to the ancestral karma system whereby you give the energies that you cannot deal with to your children, for them to deal with.

In the ensuing eons since Lucifer and Satan propagated these changes, you have learned to manage these two karmic systems. Now you have reached the point in your experience where you are ready to move beyond karma.

Therefore, this is now given to you as a choice you can make. You can choose to move out of the karmic system, and to not accumulate additional karma. The karma that you have accepted in this lifetime as part of your experience, will still need to be worked through, and released. But if you do not manage to do this in this lifetime, it will not carry forward into the next, once you have chosen to move beyond the karmic system.

When you make that choice, then your DNA starts to change. The changes instigated by Lucifer and Satan begin to roll back. The speed at which this happens is your choice. If you can truly allow yourself to release the energies of karma, then this DNA change will be instantaneous. For most people the karmic releases will take some time to complete. Therefore their DNA changes will be gradual.

We are pleased and honored to be with you at this time, and to watch how you handle these momentous changes.

The Changes to Plants and Animals

I greet you. This is Okahtier. Let us continue.

PLANET IN REBELLION

You on this planet have endured many of the impacts of moving off the intended course. One of these which the Archangels discussed above are the behavior patterns that you call human nature. Another impact has been the ways that your environment works with you. Now what I mean by this, is that the behavior of the plants and animals existing on this planet have also changed dramatically.

Before the subversion of your Planetary Prince, the idea that you could have a carnivorous plant was inconceivable. Now you take it as a rarity, and a fascinating development in evolution.

Plants, as they were originally designed for this planet, served as the base layer of energy conversion for physical form. Energy for life comes to this planet from many sources. The primary source that you are aware of is the Sun and its constant giving of energies to you and all of the planets in this solar system.

There are other less obvious forms of energy. Many of these you have defined in your occult past as subtle energies: the ethers. These energies do exist, and they are equally as important in supporting life on this planet, as are the solar radiations.

A Cosmic Look at Earth's History

How you receive these subtle energies depends upon your attunement level. There are a few yogis who exist only on the reception of these energies; they do not eat. These yogis have so attuned their bodies to the subtle energies that they take them in with every breath, and utilize them thoroughly. You also take these energies in with each breath, but your bodies are not attuned to be able to use much of them. These energies are vital to life, so you must take in some of these, but the levels that you actually use are a fraction of what is available to you.

Plants and animals also take in these subtle energies to support their lives. One of the primary functions of plants is the conversion of these energies to a form that your current bodies can use. Your food animals ingest these energies in their food, and therefore you also receive a dose of those energies from the animals that you consume.

In the distant past, when a human would consume a plant, he was capable of using all of the energies of the plant to support his/her life. Therefore there were almost no waste products from such food. With the change of energies as a result of the fall of

PLANET IN REBELLION

your Planetary Prince, this ability began to decline in humans. The energies of the plants also started changing; they began to move more and more out of sync with the energies of human beings. It was at that time that your current digestive system began to develop, and that you also began to consume animals as a food source, for you needed the greater energetic content they contained.

The animals reacted to this new relationship with humans by developing defensive techniques, and by starting to consume each other. There was indeed a time when the lion lay down with the lamb, and did not think of the lamb as dinner.

Now this planet is starting to move back into alignment with its divine position. You will find in the generations to come that the behavior of the animals will change, and that new species of plants are either discovered or developed which hold much more life force within them. You will find your eating patterns change with the desire to eat many more of these types of vegetables. And you will find that your health patterns also change as a result of this.

The Physical Changes

I greet you. This is Okahtier. I am pleased to be conversing with you once again on these topics of interest.

The question arises regarding the physical impact of this change in evolutionary paths to the human beings then alive. Just as the plants and the animals began to move out of sync with the new energies of planet, and therefore with those they were designed to support, the humans also started to move out of sync.
At that time Earth was projecting a multitude of conflicting energies. There were the loving supportive energies of the planetary soul, Gaia. There were the harsh combative energies of Satan. There were the forceful directives of Lucifer, who was moving humans to a different path of evolution. And underlying all of this were the energies of your god, Lord Michael, which were not

in harmony with the energies of either Satan or Lucifer.

Consequently those living on the planet were confused, and their bodies reflected this confusion. There were a number of ways in which this manifested. The first of these was that the physical body shape started to change. Humans became shorter as the generations progressed.

Next was the development of diseases. Life became more of a struggle as humans were no longer in harmony with the plants and animals originally designed to provide them with companionship and sustenance. Humans' bodies were receiving conflicting messages, and the food they consumed was slightly out of sync with their physical structures. This led to the development of many diseases that you still experience such as cancer and AIDS. These diseases did not exist on the planet before the dereliction of Lucifer.

A third way that humans changed is that their bodies started to degenerate as they aged, and the length of their lives decreased. This is not in the divine blueprint for the human form. Instead, what the body is

A Cosmic Look at Earth's History

supposed to do is to grow until it is mature, and then maintain that state until the human is done with his life. At that time, the human is supposed to separate easily from the body, and return to the soul that created him.

As you know well, this is not the pattern of how life is currently lived on the planet. As the planet moves into its ascension, and you gain greater understanding of what lies ahead for you after your life ends, the death process will become less of a struggle, and more the celebration it was originally designed to be.

The Loss of Off-Planet Communications

I greet you. This is Okahtier.

I will give you one more major way in which moving off of the planned path has affected life on Earth. I am sure there are many others you will be able to discover since many of you reading these materials had lives on this planet during the times we speak of. Therefore, if you compare the memories you have of how life was and should be on the planet, with how you now perceive life to be, this will give you great insight into what the potential future could be.

The last manner in which the fall of your Planetary Prince affected the life upon this planet was the cessation of communications. Before this time, you were familiar with the life that existed on planets near and far from you. You received constant communications as to their happenings, and inquiries as to what you were doing. You enjoyed hearing from them, for this planet was progressing in concert with its neighbors. Together you were working out the best ways to live in this section of the Universe with the particular conditions that all of you shared.

Once your Planetary Prince succumbed to the teachings of Lucifer, all channels of communication to and from this planet were cut. This was an abrupt cessation, which was quite a shock to those then alive. Many of you reading these materials will remember this shock, and you still feel as though you should be hearing from those neighboring planets.

    Now that you have thoroughly explored the results of moving off of the planned path, that detour is coming to an end. In the near future these communication channels will begin to be restored. At first this will appear to be chaotic, with many people starting to receive information that they do not expect. Within a fairly short amount of time, it will sort itself out, and those who can receive these communications will come to value them, and to be honored within their societies.
    We inform you of this in order to prepare you for what is coming soon.

6

THE CURRENT IMPACTS OF BEING OFF-COURSE

THE PSYCHOLOGICAL DEVELOPMENTS

I greet you. This is Okahtier.

We left our narration describing some of the physical changes that have occurred in the human race. In addition to physical changes, there have been psychological changes, some of which were described above in the Human Nature section given by the Archangels. There are additional psychological changes that I wish to cover here, and how these manifest in current times.

The first of these is an expansion of the discussion on aggression given by the Archangels. This frequently manifests itself within your current cultures as a constant battling for position. Such competitiveness is believed to be an appropriate and proper way to live. You teach your children this by teaching them to compete in school for grades, and to compete on the sports fields. However, this competitiveness frequently escalates to warfare between groups or countries.

This pattern of behavior is now nearing the end of its usefulness to you. You can see this in the beliefs that now abound that a soldier should not be injured or die in a battle. Despite the fact that this is what the soldier has signed up to do, it is now believed that this should not happen.

The next point that I wish to cover is that of a certain type of powerlessness that many of you experience. You do not believe that you have any power to act effectively against any of your social structures. This is exemplified in your approach to your corporations. You believe that they are stronger than you are. In fact, your corporations just reflect the beliefs of the masses, of which you are one element. You are a conscious piece of this, and most of the masses are still unconscious. This means that your input has far more power to cause changes in the directions you desire, if you just stick with the positive beliefs.

The last point that I wish to discuss is your beliefs in the necessity to conform to your current social structures. You believe that you are tied into these social relationships, and that these ties make you unable to act freely in creative ways. In short, they stifle your freedom. A very deep part of you that desires your happiness has been sending you urges to act in ways that do not conform, but are not illegal. These impulses you have suppressed and ignored. If you could begin to express these in small ways, then you will start to see paths open up that will lead you toward ways of living that are much more in alignment with who you are.

THE SUBCONSCIOUS KNOWLEDGE OF GOD

We greet you. We are the Hosts of Heaven. We are honored to be sharing some of our experiences and knowledge with you now.

Lucifer had moved the planet to a new and unique course. This is a path that very few planets have survived. There are not many that have been taken to this place. Therefore we are fascinated to see and document how Earth has managed to navigate this morass.

As you have been told, this planet was headed into chaos, which manifested on all levels of your design. Emotionally, it manifested as depression and the constant warfare that you are so familiar with. Physically, it manifested as degeneration of the physical form. Mentally, it manifested as the ivory tower syndrome, where people get locked in their heads, with no references to a physical world. And spiritually, it has manifest as confusion and religious one-upmanship.

As a result, we who are your constant companions needed to find a way to stabilize you. The direction we chose was to create a subconscious level within the human being that contained the knowledge of your connection to God. Every cell within your body holds this knowledge. It is this knowledge that physically supports and sustains you in all of your trials. It is this knowledge that gives you the degree of health that you have enjoyed until now. We needed to hide this information within you in order for the knowledge to survive.

Now this knowledge is starting to rise into your consciousness; it is starting to move from your subconscious to your awareness. It is bringing much confusion with it as it does so. You have truly believed that you were isolated and abandoned here on this planet, and you were not.

Now that this wisdom is starting to rise up, you can help it by learning to enjoy the sheer beauty of this planet, and therefore of your life. If you can spend just five minutes a day immersed in this enjoyment, you will find your wisdom has a much easier time integrating into your consciousness.

Interesting and Unexpected Results

I greet you. I am Saint Germain. I wish to cover this section.

There have been a number of interesting and unexpected results from the levels of depravity to which Lucifer's followers led you. These results are not something that we foresaw.

You, as a race, have managed to develop totally unexpected levels of compassion and forgiveness as a result of your concentrated exploration of the depths of emotions. Most recently, you can see this in the life of Mother Theresa, who demonstrated the love of her

God in the bowels of abject poverty. The ability to do this is an unexpected result of your experiences.

Another development that I wish to cover are the ways and directions in which your children are developing. Your children are moving ahead in their changes much more quickly than we anticipated. We expected that the race would take a hundred years or more to show the results we have seen in your children in the last decade. You, as race, no longer desire to repeat the past, and therefore you are pushing ahead full steam.
These new developments are aimed at creating the ability to live multi-dimensionally upon this planet. You see this in children who cannot organize information in linear ways, and indeed they cannot. But very soon they will figure out how to present multi-dimensional information to their linear parents, and then they will begin to thrive in your schools and in your workplaces.

The third development that I wish to discuss is one that the race is currently developing. You will see this first in your very young children. They will not lose this ability as they grow up, and eventually they will be able to teach this to their parents. And this ability is to conceptually span all levels of experience, from the greatest depths to the heights of God.

This will be a mental ability that flies in the face of what Lucifer sought to do with this race. Lucifer tried to confine you to the mental realms, because he believed that it was easier to control you there. This is part of the reason so much of your current culture worships the mind. You have taken this restraint, and brought it to God, and brought God to it. This is most unexpected.

The last point I wish to cover is one that discusses the actual evolutionary path you are now on. This path was designed to dead-end you into a form of servitude, and it has served this function well for the eons since Lucifer placed the planet on it. Now you are taking that path, and using it to leapfrog your evolution.

On the evolutionary path designed for Earth, you would be nowhere near the levels of development that you are now approaching.

PLANET IN REBELLION

You would be about one-third of the way to where you are now. The path would have been much more enjoyable, but also much longer. Now the planet is starting to move into its ascension, eons earlier than originally planned. Therefore you have managed to take the path given you by Lucifer and use it to propel yourselves far ahead of where you would have been had you taken the original path.

For this, and all of these unexpected results, I congratulate you.

7

Moving to the Present

The Corruption of Lucifer

We greet you. We are the Hosts of Heaven. We will pick up the narration at this point.

As you have been informed, Lucifer's original teachings were aimed at shortcutting the ascension process for this planet. This planet was designed to allow a great deal of flexibility in how it chose to evolve. Lucifer took this flexibility and began to bend it to his plan.

PLANET IN REBELLION

What Lucifer was not aware of was that in doing so, he cut himself off from several types of subtle energies that are provided by the Creator to all of Creation that is in alignment with him. By attempting to shortcut the divine plan for this planet, Lucifer placed himself outside of alignment with the Creator.

The loss of this particular type of connection can be very subtle. You have experienced it as having a certain gleam of joy go out of your experience. You eventually notice the lack of this sparkle, and you then try many different types of experiences to get it back. And this is what Lucifer did. He did not notice at first that the effervescence had departed, but eventually the lack built up to the point that he noticed it. Then he began to do as you do, to try to get it back.

It would have been relatively easy for Lucifer to regain his former level of light at that point if he had been willing to give up the path he was promoting on this planet and elsewhere. Unfortunately, by that time Lucifer's pride was invested in his project, and he refused to change direction. Therefore, his vibrational rate began to fall more quickly. This left Lucifer open to the low vibrational forces that do exist within Creation. Most of these forces are entities created in the far distant past when the vibrational rate of all of Creation was much lower. They still reflect the vibrational levels at which they were created, and when an entity falls within the range they can access, they will use the energies of that entity for themselves. Lucifer's vibrational rate fell to those levels.

    As a result, Lucifer sought to bring the energetic levels of the planets where he had influence to his new low levels; he began to turn his focus toward the actions that would lower the vibrational rate of all those planets. He instructed Satan and his minions in new techniques that would try to lock the planet into those lower energetic levels.

    Lucifer was still a physically beautiful and brilliant being. Therefore, it was difficult for many beings to see that he had turned toward a darker focus. There were many within your solar system who continued to follow Lucifer down his new path. We lost approximately one quarter of the beings who were assigned to this planet to Lucifer. All of them were relieved of their duties. Many have since repented, gone through a rehabilitation program, and been assigned to tasks elsewhere. None of them are still here with this planet.

However, there was a period before these followers of Lucifer were relieved of their duties. During that time period, which is before your recorded history, those living on the planet devolved. You do not have records of the heights of civilization that were reached before this dramatic downturn. There were many long lasting, peaceful and beautiful societies before that time. The records that you do have, including the records contained within your myths, legends, and religious texts, start with the time in which the race finally began to stabilize after the intense warfare involved in the period of devolvement. You remember a bit of this in your legends of the fall of Atlantis.

We will leave the narration at this point, and turn the document over to Gaia.

Becoming a Planet of Free Will

I greet you. This is Gaia.

I must admit that having the Planetary Prince succumb to the blandishments of Lucifer was quite a shock to me. The changes that the Planetary Prince and Lucifer introduced to the populations living on this planet was a change in direction from what I had been working on implementing.

Changes that are made to the surface and to the peoples on the planet directly affect my wellbeing. You could describe the attendant feelings as a toothache for a tooth that you cannot pull. Therefore, I began to look at the probable futures for the planet, and I was dismayed at what I was seeing. In most, if not almost all of the futures, all life on the planet ceased in fairly short order. There was a small group of improbable futures that I could see which involved changing the direction and the nature of this planet. Therefore, I chose to throw open the doors of chance, and to become a planet of free will.

PLANET IN REBELLION

Because of your familiarity with free will, you also do not realize that this planet was not originally intended to be a planet of free will. It was intended to explore the very complicated four body system in a structured manner. Instead, what you have done is explore the four body system in a free-for-all evolutionary system.

You know well the structures and tenants of a planet of free will, as this is all you have known throughout your recorded history. You understand how to move through these types of decisions, and how to raise your children to make appropriate choices. You would be surprised to discover that being a planet of free will is very unusual within the universe. There are very few of them, and there are fewer still that have managed to negotiate this freedom of choice to reach a point in which a planet will ascend.

I made this decision to become a planet of free will 100,000 years ago. This is the time period that the Kryon discusses when the Pleiadians gifted you with the appropriate DNA to allow this. The Pleiadians gave you this gift at my request. I selected them because

I believed that their way of enabling free choice was less subject to being corrupted by Lucifer, Satan and their minions who were still highly active on the planet and somewhat in control.

The Pleiadians have achieved physical mastery of free choice. Therefore their gift to you is the physical gift of free will. I believed that the other aspects of the four body system were too easy to overwhelm or corrupt, and my choice has proven to be resilient as you are moving out of the influences of Lucifer's teachings.

THE FOUR BODIES AND FREE WILL

We greet you. We are the Hosts of Heaven.

The design of human beings on this planet involves an implementation of the four body system. Gaia could have chosen to implement free will in any one of these four points of view. She chose the physical element for the reasons discussed above.

PLANET IN REBELLION

You have been gifted with physical free choice. This means that you can go anywhere to do anything. Physicality leads the choice. To a very large degree your societies have sought to constrain your physical ability to move freely. This is what your property laws are, and most of the laws within your books.

You have much less ability to see or to move emotionally. Many of you get stuck in particular emotions, and cannot see any way of moving these. You do not have an innate ability to move emotions at will, or in particular directions. Instead you must let them play out until they release their energies. And while this represents a type of movement, it is not the movement of free will.

As for your mental configurations, this is similar to the emotional. Many of you can get easily locked into particular mental interpretations of the world. Once you are locked into this, you cannot easily find ways out. Therefore you do not have free choice about mental movements.

You have not had an active access to your innate spiritual abilities in some time. This is one of the first things that Lucifer sought to disconnect. As a result, this point of view was not available for Gaia to choose.

You can always choose to physically move. This is so familiar to you that you do not see how this may not be the case on other planets. And while physicality is one of your slower paths to enlightenment, it still is a necessary part of any path to enlightenment.

This is not the case on other worlds. They can reach enlightenment without engaging the physical at all. You cannot.

THE GIFT OF FREE WILL

We greet you. We are the Hosts of Heaven. We desire to present the next section.

At the time we are discussing, evolution had stopped upon this planet. The planet had descended into a state of fairly constant warfare, with small tribes battling one another, and battling any that came from the outside to either help them or to hurt them.

PLANET IN REBELLION

Because they could not tell the difference between those of us who came from Lord Michael, and those who came from Lucifer, they chose to assume that all those they did not personally know, intended to bring them into servitude and pain. Therefore, all attempts to draw humans out of that state of being failed. As an aside, we desire to tell you that the human ability to continually fight the minions of Lucifer is highly unusual among the planets that succumbed to Lucifer's teachings. Most of the other planets fell into line fairly quickly, and have remained in servitude since then.

It was at that time that Gaia threw open the doors of her planet to free will. When she chose this, it seemed to us to be an ambitious and difficult choice. Why would she choose free will when the current will of those on the planet was being used to defend their small fiefdoms?

We, as your constant companions, do not have access to the particular types of information that Gaia has. Gaia is the planet, and therefore she can see the future of the planet in ways that we cannot. We are your companions. We can see the potentials of your individual futures, but we cannot aggregate these futures in the ways Gaia can. And therefore we chose to trust that Gaia knew what she was doing.

As Gaia had chosen the Pleiadians to deliver the gift, the Pleiadians began to move among you at that time. Mostly they chose to appear only to the one who directly received their gift, and frequently they appeared in a disguised form. Their offering to those persons was the gift of the particular DNA needed to enable physical free will. Those who received their gift thrived in their tribes. Many of them became leaders of their groups. Because of their enhanced DNA, those leaders could see other ways for the tribe to behave that benefited their groups. Thus evolution once again started, but from a diminished level.

Once Gaia implemented this gift of free will, our duties began to change in regard to you, our companions. We became much more to you than we had been before. We moved into a new role for us, which was to be your educators, your teachers in the ways of navigating the new gift of free will. Even now, you can call upon us for emotional and psychological support, as many of you do. This was our intended role in your lives.

But now you can also call upon us when you desire teachings of a particular nature. For example, you desire teachings on how to interact with your bodies in a more mutually beneficial manner. You can call upon us to help educate both you and your body so that this interaction will be mutually effective. We desire that you expand your concepts of who we, the Archangels, are in order to enable these types of interactions.

The Dream Schools

We greet you. We are the Hosts of Heaven.

We left off this narration where the planet had fallen into a form of subjugation. There are many entities here on this side of the veil who sought means to bring you out of this servitude. Many different techniques were tried. The means that has proven to be the most successful is enhancing the free-will abilities that Gaia had arranged for you to be given.

As we have mentioned above, we are your constant companions, and we were tasked with helping you understand how free will could be used to raise your level of well-being. By that time the races were in decline. Physical diseases were rampant, the levels of warfare between tribes was high, and therefore the death rate in the fairly small population on the planet was also high.

It was at that time that we began our implementation of dream schools for humans. Many of you remember these in their heyday. There you met those you would come to trust in other tribes before you physically met the other tribes. There you learned what plants and animals you could safely eat. There is where you first met your domestic animals. And there is where you learned how to harness the fire from lightning to cook your food.

You will notice from the list given above, that most of what we taught you in those dream schools was how and where to physically move in order to enhance your lives. This was because you had been gifted with physical free will.

PLANET IN REBELLION

Once your physical well-being was assured, then you had time and energy to start to develop the other aspects of the four body system. Your development of your mental abilities within the last five hundred years has been astounding.

You have taken races that were under spiritual subjugation and used your mental capacities to break them free. Now that this is assured, you have the time and energy to look back over the spiritual side of your being, and to revamp those abilities. You will find, in the next hundred years, an explosion of understanding of the spiritual side of your lives. We look forward to being your companions on that exploration.

The Development of the Religions

I greet you. This is your Lord Michael. I will continue these materials.

A Cosmic Look at Earth's History

As Gaia has said, the plan for the evolution of Earth was in abeyance; it was no longer possible to implement it. Therefore we needed to wait and see exactly what human beings would make of that new path before we could start to plan for any sort of spiritual advancement. It was many long years that we waited before we could determine how to best assist this planet in coming out of the darkness to which it descended. You recollect much of that time period as this is all of your recorded history, and much of your prehistory described by your anthropologists.

It became clear approximately three thousand years ago which directions those living upon the planet were choosing. Therefore with that information, I chose to start bringing in different types of support than I had previously supplied. As a result, quite a number of spiritual leaders began to be born to all of the tribes that could support them. This occurred in all of the races on the planet.

Those that I chose to become your spiritual leaders were souls who had "been through the fires" so to speak, and had shown themselves able to maintain their levels of connection to me in those circumstances. We also worked to give those humans a greater level of connection beyond the veil, so they could anchor the teachings that the planet was ready to accept.

In the western world, the main teacher that you now follow is Jesus. The Christians are descendants of the Jewish religion, which spiritually begins with the teachings of Moses. In the eastern world, many follow Buddha, but there are also other influences present from previous teachers such as Lao Tzu and Confucius. Those teachers sought to increase your levels of understanding and connections to me, bit by bit. The particular format that they chose for each religion depended upon the culture and spiritual levels of the time and place.

If you search, you will find that at the core level, there is very little difference between the teachings of the various religions. All of them sought to teach you the experience of existing within the love that permeates and underlies all of Creation. All of them, at their inception, taught that you are valued, you are loved and you are important to Creation. And all of them taught ways of extending the love that you could feel outward to your neighbors.

All of the religions, at their core, provided a very potent way of connecting to the love of the Creator. All of the religions, at the time of their origin, taught techniques that would quickly and directly lead their followers into unmistakable experiences of that love.

Since then, most of these techniques have either been forgotten, hidden, distorted, or perverted, so that what remains is just a shell. The loss of those techniques was deliberate on the part of those who followed Lucifer. These religions were seen by Lucifer's followers as a very potent threat when they were first revealed by their founders.

As you well know with your current experience with the religions, those attempts to lose these techniques were somewhat successful. You have Christians proclaiming they have the only way to God, you have Muslims willing to kill anyone who questions their particular interpretation of the Koran, and you have Buddhists who seek to withdraw from the world into their own personal nirvana. However, the core materials for many of these religions still exist, and will be rediscovered soon. Once your scholars lose the biases which currently inform their understandings, these materials will be found in plain sight. At that point, your religions will begin to return to the vision provided by their founders.

Nevertheless, you have responded well to those teachings. As a result, the spiritual level of the planet has grown by leaps and bounds. It may sound strange to you that we can actually measure the level of spiritual understanding that those on the planet exhibit, but we can. And I tell you now that the levels of this understanding have continued to grow at a faster and faster rate over the last several thousand years. Now that Lucifer, his minion Satan, and your former Planetary Prince are blocked from acting here, you have taken this opportunity to grow your understandings exponentially. And the rate of increase is continuing to rise as we speak.

You passed the tipping point of no return in this at the end of 2012, with the inauguration of the new age. Therefore, in the times to come you can expect to finally see the world that you have long desired.

8

Anticipation of the Future

Transitioning to the New Energies

I greet you. This is Gaia. I will continue.

As we have narrated, there was a design and plan for this planet that it is no longer following. Instead, what those living on this planet have chosen to do is, in effect, to take the shortcut offered by Lucifer, and implement it in their own fashion. This means that you have taken all of the distortions and downright cruelty propagated by those such as Satan and your Planetary Prince and managed to turn them into something marvelous. With the change of ages at the end of 2012, we have moved into new energies, and a new way of relating to each other. True, you are not yet seeing the effects of this change of energies, but you are feeling the effects of it in the disruption and decay of your social and financial structures.

This transition of energies does not have to be difficult for you, personally. You can choose to consciously and unconsciously align with the new energies. When you choose to do this with all of yourself, all of your being, then you will find that things magically happen for you in ways that you cannot anticipate.

This is what you have called here to this planet, now. You have been tired of the repetition of the old patterns of aggression and sorrow, and thus you have asked for new and different patterns of living. And these are here now for you to grasp, use and enjoy.

PLANET IN REBELLION

The End of Quarantine

We greet you. We are the Hosts of Heaven. We will present this section.

As we have mentioned above, your planet is beginning its movement out of quarantine. There are a couple of reasons for this.
The first of these is that the planet has chosen to ascend, and to bring all those alive upon it along in the process. In the beginning, this requirement is slowing down the process of the planet's ascension. Once the planet gets through the initial phases, the desire to bring everyone along works to speed up the process. This is because you will have the aid and assistance of your families, friends and neighbors while you are undergoing the process. With this broad base of support, you will be much more willing to move through it quickly. As everyone will be going through it, there will be many different techniques created to assist those who are having difficulties with the process.

We know those who discover and read this material have not found this to be the case in their experiences. Those who find this material within the first twenty years of its publication are the forerunners for the general population. While it has been difficult being a forerunner, it is also exhilarating. If you look at your experiences carefully, you will discover this has been the case. You should take pride in your abilities and your status as a forerunner.

The second reason is that you have finally navigated all the pathways and experiences introduced by Lucifer, Satan and their followers. When you reach the end of an experience, it closes, and a new one opens. This is similar to what you experience when you graduate from school. The old experience of teachers and classes closes, and the new experiences of what you do with what you have learned opens. This is what the planet is going through in its ascension process, the closing of the past, and the opening of a wonderful future that contains everything that you have desired.

Now, the question arises; what will you experience when the planet moves out of quarantine?

As discussed above, there are a variety of connections this planet had to the wider universe which have been inactive since the planet fell to Lucifer. Among these are the reduction in the energies provided by the Creator to support life, the blocking of communications with your neighboring planets, and the cessation of the delivery of spiritual energies to the planet. Once the planet is taken out of quarantine, all of these will resume.

You may experience the resumption of communications as finally locating radio signals that denote life on other planets, or as mentally receiving information (this is also called telepathy). Your children will experience the greater energies that support life through much longer lifespans than you currently have. You may experience this as a sudden reversal of some disease you have.

The increased spiritual energies also will be seen as a resurgence of the religions. This resurgence will be presented as that which the founders of the religions sought to invoke in their followers. Therefore, you will see the religions presenting themselves as forces of true love, and choosing to cooperate with each other instead of competing as they now do.

9

THE RETURN TO THE DIVINE PATH

I greet you. This is your Lord Michael. I am pleased to be talking with you now about this most important subject.

As related to you earlier, the planet has come far in its endeavors to throw off the misunderstandings brought about by the teachings of Lucifer. Your planet has taken a very unexpected route to its current position, one of thoroughly understanding the effects of those particular forms of rebellion from the love of the Creator. As a result, Earth now moves past its rebellion and begins its return to a divine path.

This path that you are now moving toward is one that you have chosen; it is not one that I chose or that I designed for you. This new path brings with it much greatness and glory. It brings with it a vast amount of compassion, and an understanding of many different and unique ways of assisting other planets through their woes. For this is what many of you will chose to do when you finally chose to leave this planet for the last time; you will chose to move on to one of the many other planets within Creation that desire your knowledge and assistance in raising themselves out of their issues and into the light of love.

Therefore, I desire that you learn to celebrate that which you have learned and accomplished. Although the path to this point has been difficult, you have broken through. You will begin to see all that you have desired for so many long years starting to appear in your lives. You will begin to see your children and grandchildren celebrating the lives that they have, in ways you could not. And when you return to this planet, you will live lives of celebration in ways you have not dared to dream possible.

Above and beyond all, I truly congratulate you on this accomplishment. I welcome you back into the love of the Creator, and I truly desire for you to experience this fully in all that you do and live.

All my love.

A Cosmic Look at Earth's History

INDEX

A

Ancestral karma 49
Animals, change 51-55
Archangels 12, 45, 51, 59-60, 79 (See Hosts of Heaven)

B

Blueprint (for evolution) 18, 25-26, 41, 55

C

Communications, Off-Planet 8, 57-58, 91
Creator 14-15, 20, 25, 28-29, 34, 39, 42, 69, 84, 91, 94-95

D

Divine path 39, 93-94
Dream schools 79-80

F

Four body system 20, 73-74, 81
Free will 36, 72   Development of 78, 80

G

Gaia (See Mother Nature) 12, 14, 20, 25, 31, 43, 54, 71-72, 74, 76-78, 80, 82, 87
god 13, 17, 25, 37, 39, 44, 54
God 25, 34, 62-63, 65-66, 84

H

Hosts of Heaven 12, 45, 62, 68, 74, 76, 79, 89 (See Archangels)
Human nature 45-47, 51, 59

K

Karma 48-50
Karma, ancestral 49
Kryon 73

L

Lord Michael 13, 17, 25, 27-28, 31, 35, 40, 54, 77, 81, 93
Lucifer 8, 14, 25, 27-30, 32-38, 40-41, 43, 48-50, 54-55, 57, 62, 64, 66-72, 74-75, 77, 84-85, 87, 90-91, 93

M

Mother Nature (See Gaia) 12, 25

N

New energies 54, 87-88

O

Okahtier 14, 24, 36, 40, 43, 48, 50, 54, 56, 59

P

Physical Changes 50, 54

Planetary Design 17
Planetary Prince 25, 27, 36-41, 43, 51, 53, 57, 72, 85, 88
Plants, changes 51-55, 80
Pleiadians 73-74, 78
Psychological developments/changes 59-60, 79

Q

Quarantine 8, 41, 89, 91

R

Religion, Development of 81
Religions 22, 25, 81, 83, 84, 85, 91, 92

S

Satambuseeno 15, 33, 35
Satan 29, 48-50, 54-55, 70, 74, 85, 88, 90
St. Germain 16

V

Vywamus 21

www.ingramcontent.com/pod-product-compliance
Lightning Source LLC
Chambersburg PA
CBHW070653050426
42451CB00008B/335